# Little Math Stories

# Add It Up

## By Amanda Gebhardt

2

# How many? How much?

Just add it up.

 Add up this.

# Add up that.

**Add this snack.**

**Add that stick.**

8 Add up blocks.

Add up rocks.

Add them flat.

Stack them up.

 Set them in six big bins.

If Meg asks how many, how much, just remember to add it up.

## math words

| | |
|---|---|
| add | much |
| many | six |

## sight words

| | |
|---|---|
| how | remember |
| How | to |
| many | |

## consonant digraphs

| /ch/ ch | /k/ ck | /d/ dd | /th/ th |
|---|---|---|---|
| much | blocks | add | that |
| | rocks | | them |
| | snack | | this |
| | Stack | | |
| | stick | | |

## Try It!

Add up the items in one of the pictures.
How many are there?

How many? How much?
Just add it up.
Add up this.
Add up that.
Add this snack.
Add that stick.
Add up blocks.
Add up rocks.
Add them flat.
Stack them up.
Set them in six big bins.
If Meg asks how many, how much,
    just remember to add it up.

CHERRY BLOSSOM PRESS

Published in the United States of America by Cherry Lake Publishing Group
Ann Arbor, Michigan
www.cherrylakepublishing.com

Photo Credits: Cover: © Aprescindere/Dreamstime.com; pages 2-4, 10-11, 13, 15: © Monkey Business Images/Dreamstime.com; page 5: © Studio.G photography/Shutterstock.com; page 6: © TetianaRUD/Shutterstock.com; page 7: © SUKJAI PHOTO/Shutterstock.com; page 8: © myboys.me/Shutterstock.com; page 9: © CROSX/Shutterstock.com; page 12: © SchubPhoto/Shutterstock.com; Back Cover: © FabrikaSimf/Shutterstock.com

**Cherry Blossom Press** is an imprint of Cherry Lake Publishing Group.

Library of Congress Cataloging-in-Publication Data has been filed and is available at catalog.loc.gov.

Cherry Lake Publishing Group would like to acknowledge the work of the Partnership for 21st Century Learning, a Network of Battelle for Kids. Please visit http://www.battelleforkids.org/networks/p21 for more information.

Printed in the United States of America
Corporate Graphics

**Amanda Gebhardt** is a curriculum writer and editor and a life-long learner. She lives in Ann Arbor, Michigan, with her husband, two kids, and one playful pup named Cookie.